General Instructio

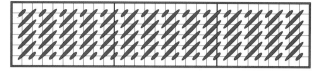

Base Assembly

For each stocking holder, in addition to the pieces shown with the instructions for each design, cut the following pieces from clear plastic canvas:

For back base: two sides and one each of top, bottom, front and back.

For front base: two sides and one each of top, bottom, front and back.

Stitch base pieces following patterns on graphs, using the following colors:

- Burgundy for Santa
- Light sage for snowman
- Soft navy for angel
- Mid brown for bear
- Warm brown for gingerbread man

When stitching is completed, for each base, Whipstitch top, bottom and front together. Whipstitch one side in place, then Whipstitch back in place.

Fill front base with one cup aquarium gravel and back base with two cups aquarium gravel.

Whipstitch remaining side for each base in place.

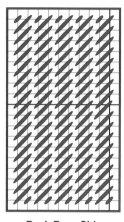

Front Base Front & Back
29 holes x 6 holes
Cut 2 from clear

Back Base Side
11 holes x 19 holes
Cut 2 from clear

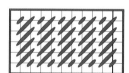

Front Base Side
11 holes x 6 holes
Cut 2 from clear

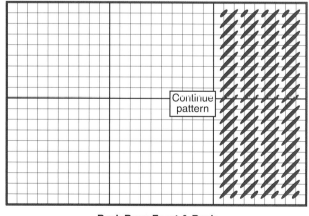

Continue pattern

Back Base Front & Back
29 holes x 19 holes
Cut 2 from clear

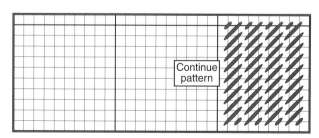

Continue pattern

Front Base Top & Bottom
29 holes x 11 holes
Cut 2 from clear

Back Base Top & Bottom
29 holes x 11 holes
Cut 2 from clear

Santa

Size: 6⅞ inches W x 7¾ inches H 3⅞ inches D
(17.5cm x 19.7cm x 9.8cm)
Skill Level: Intermediate

Materials

- ❏ 2 sheets clear 7-count plastic canvas
- ❏ ½ sheet dark green 7-count plastic canvas
- ❏ Red Heart Super Saver Art. E300 medium weight yarn as listed in color key
- ❏ Red Heart Classic Art. E267 medium weight yarn as listed in color key
- ❏ #16 tapestry needle
- ❏ ⅝-inch (1.6cm) yellow-gold star button
- ❏ 3 (5mm) red beads
- ❏ Small amount dark red felt
- ❏ 1½-inch (38mm) brass S hook
- ❏ 3 cups aquarium gravel
- ❏ Hot-glue gun

Stitching Step by Step

1 Following graphs (pages 3, 4 and 5) throughout instructions, cut tree and holly leaves from dark green plastic canvas; cut Santa front, back, beard, mustache, mittens, tree trunk and bag handle from clear plastic canvas. Santa back will remain unstitched.

2 Cut nose and mouth from dark red felt using patterns given (page 5).

3 Stitch and assemble base pieces with burgundy, following General Instructions.

4 Backstitch holly leaves; do not Overcast. Using white, work Lark's Head Knots (page 5) for beard; trim to desired length. (Each length on sample is trimmed to approximately 1-inch/2.5cm.) Do not Overcast beard.

5 Stitch Santa front, working Continental Stitches in uncoded areas as follows: white background with burgundy, beige background with buff. Stitch and Overcast remaining pieces.

6 When background stitching is completed, work black Backstitches for eyebrows and gold Backstitches to outline white trim on Santa's coat.

7 Whipstitch Santa front and back together.

Assembly

1 Use photo as a guide throughout assembly. Glue holly leaves to hat; glue red beads in a cluster at bottom of leaves.

2 Glue bag handle in place on right side of Santa. Glue one mitten over handle at bottom of arm.

3 Place beard, mouth, mustache and nose on face; glue in place in the order given.

4 Glue star button to top of tree and top of trunk to center back at bottom of tree. Glue tree to Santa, then glue remaining mitten in place at bottom of arm over tree trunk.

5 Center and glue Santa between front and back bases, making sure bottom edges are even.

6 Insert S hook in front center hole of base front top.

COLOR KEY

Yards	Medium Weight Yarn
4 (3.7m)	☐ White #311
2 (1.9m)	■ Black #312
1 (1m)	☐ Gold #321
1 (1m)	☐ Warm brown #336
1 (1m)	☐ Paddy green #368
1 (1m)	☐ Petal pink #373
4 (3.7m)	☐ Hunter green #389
1 (1m)	☐ Skipper blue #848
3 (2.8m)	Uncoded area on beige background is buff #334
41 (37.5m)	Uncoded areas on white background are burgundy #376 Continental Stitches
	✏ Burgundy #376 Overcast and Whipstitch
1 (1m)	✏ Light gray #341 Overcast
	✏ Black #312 Backstitch
	✏ Gold #321 Backstitch
	✏ Hunter green #389 Backstitch
	○ White #311 Lark's Head Knot

Color numbers given are for Red Heart Super Saver Art. E300 and Classic Art. E267 medium weight yarn.

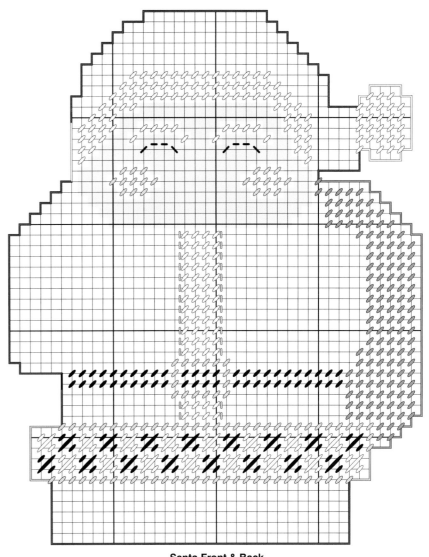

Santa Front & Back
40 holes x 50 holes
Cut 2 from clear
Stitch front only

Tree
16 holes x 16 holes
Cut 1 from dark green

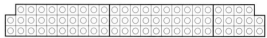

Beard
25 holes x 3 holes
Cut 1 from clear

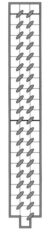

Bag Handle
3 holes x 21 holes
Cut 1 from clear

Mitten
7 holes x 7 holes
Cut 2 from clear

Tree Trunk
2 holes x 11 holes
Cut 1 from clear

Holly Leaf
4 holes x 4 holes
Cut 2 from dark green

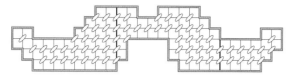

Mustache
26 holes x 6 holes
Cut 1 from clear

Nose
Cut 1 from
dark red felt

Mouth
Cut 1 from dark red felt

Lark's Head Knot

COLOR KEY	
Yards	**Medium Weight Yarn**
4 (3.7m)	☐ White #311
2 (1.9m)	■ Black #312
1 (1m)	☐ Gold #321
1 (1m)	☐ Warm brown #336
1 (1m)	☐ Paddy green #368
1 (1m)	☐ Petal pink #373
4 (3.7m)	■ Hunter green #389
1 (1m)	■ Skipper blue #848
3 (2.8m)	Uncoded area on beige background is buff #334
41 (37.5m)	Uncoded areas on white background are burgundy #376 Continental Stitches
	✐ Burgundy #376 Overcast and Whipstitch
1 (1m)	✐ Light gray #341 Overcast
	✐ Black #312 Backstitch
	✐ Gold #321 Backstitch
	✐ Hunter green #389 Backstitch
	○ White #311 Lark's Head Knot

Color numbers given are for Red Heart Super Saver Art. E300 and Classic Art. E267 medium weight yarn.

Snowman

Size: 6¼ inches W x 7⅜ inches H x 3⅞ inches D
(15.9cm x 18.7cm x 9.8cm)
Skill Level: Intermediate

Materials

- ❑ 2 sheets 7-count plastic canvas
- ❑ Red Heart Super Saver Art. E300 medium weight yarn as listed in color key
- ❑ Red Heart Classic Art. E267 medium weight yarn as listed in color key
- ❑ #16 tapestry needle
- ❑ Hand-sewing needle
- ❑ 2 (¼-inch/0.6cm) round black buttons
- ❑ 3 (⁷⁄₁₆-inch/1.1cm) round black buttons
- ❑ ¾-inch (1.9cm) gold heart button
- ❑ Small amount orange felt
- ❑ 1½-inch (3.8cm) brass S hook
- ❑ 3 cups aquarium gravel
- ❑ Hot-glue gun

Stitching Step by Step

1 Following graphs (pages 7 and 8) throughout instructions, cut snowman front, back, mitten, birdhouse and birdhouse roof from plastic canvas (pages 7 and 8). Snowman back and birdhouse back will remain unstitched.

2 Cut nose from orange felt using pattern given (page 7).

3 Stitch and assemble base pieces with light sage, following General Instructions.

4 Stitch snowman and birdhouse front pieces, working Continental Stitches in uncoded areas as follows: white background with white, blue background with country blue. Stitch and Overcast remaining pieces.

5 When background stitching is completed, work embroidery with floss as follows: black Backstitches for mouth, dark blue Backstitches to outline scarf, and tan Cross Stitches on patchwork.

6 Use hand-sewing needle and black embroidery floss to attach ¼-inch/0.6cm buttons and ⁷⁄₁₆-inch/1.1cm buttons where indicated on graph.

7 Whipstitch snowman front and back together; work Lark's Head Knots (page 7) for scarf fringe with country blue; trim to desired length. (Lengths on sample are trimmed to approximately 1 inch/2.5cm.)

8 Whipstitch birdhouse front and back together.

Assembly

1 Use photo as a guide throughout assembly. Glue birdhouse roof to top of birdhouse. Glue birdhouse to snowman and heart button to center front of birdhouse.

2 Glue mitten over birdhouse pole at bottom of arm.

3 Glue nose to head.

4 Center and glue snowman between front and back bases, making sure bottom edges are even.

5 Insert S hook in front center hole of base front top.

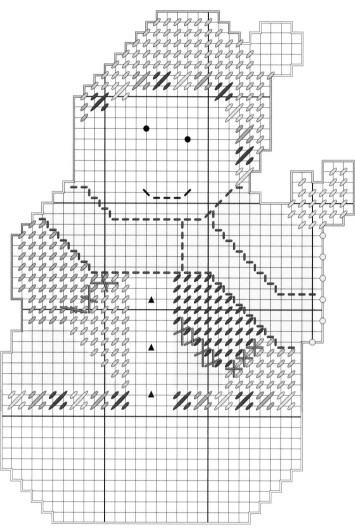

Snowman Front & Back
34 holes x 48 holes
Cut 2
Stitch front only

COLOR KEY

Yards	Medium Weight Yarn
2 (1.9m)	☐ Gold #321
2 (1.9m)	☐ Warm brown #336
4 (3.7m)	■ Burgundy #376
6 (5.5m)	☐ Country blue #382
2 (1.9m)	▨ Soft navy #387
35 (32m)	▨ Light sage #631
7 (6.5m)	Uncoded areas on white background are white #311 Continental Stitches
	Uncoded areas on blue background are country blue #382 Continental Stitches
	⁄ White #311 Whipstitch
	○ Country blue #382 Lark's Head Knot

6-Strand Embroidery Floss

3 (2.8m)	⁄ Dark blue Backstitch
2 (1.9m)	⁄ Black Backstitch
2 (1.9m)	✖ Tan Cross Stitch
	● Attach ¼-inch (0.6cm) button
	▲ Attach ⁷⁄₁₆-inch (1.1cm) button

Color numbers given are for Red Heart Super Saver Art. E300 and Classic Art. E267 medium weight yarn.

Nose
Cut 1 from
orange felt

Lark's Head Knot

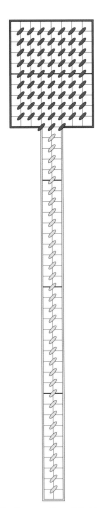

Birdhouse Front & Back
8 holes x 45 holes
Cut 2
Stitch front only

Mitten
6 holes x 6 holes
Cut 1

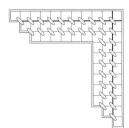

Birdhouse Roof
11 holes x 11 holes
Cut 1

COLOR KEY	
Yards	**Medium Weight Yarn**
2 (1.9m)	☐ Gold #321
2 (1.9m)	☐ Warm brown #336
4 (3.7m)	■ Burgundy #376
6 (5.5m)	☐ Country blue #382
2 (1.9m)	■ Soft navy #387
35 (32m)	☐ Light sage #631
7 (6.5m)	Uncoded areas on white background are white #311 Continental Stitches Uncoded areas on blue background are country blue #382 Continental Stitches
	⁄ White #311 Whipstitch
	○ Country blue #382 Lark's Head Knot
	6-Strand Embroidery Floss
3 (2.8m)	⁄ Dark blue Backstitch
2 (1.9m)	⁄ Black Backstitch
2 (1.9m)	✖ Tan Cross Stitch
	● Attach ¼-inch (0.6cm) button
	▲ Attach 7/16-inch (1.1cm) button

Color numbers given are for Red Heart Super Saver Art. E300 and Classic Art. E267 medium weight yarn.

Angel

Size: 7¼ inches W x 7¾ inches H x 3⅞ inches D
(18.4cm x 19.7cm x 9.8cm)

Skill Level: Intermediate

Materials

- ❑ 2 sheets 7-count plastic canvas
- ❑ Red Heart Classic Art. E267 medium weight yarn as listed in color key
- ❑ Red Heart Super Saver Art. E300 medium weight yarn as listed in color key
- ❑ 6-strand embroidery floss as listed in color key
- ❑ #16 tapestry needle
- ❑ Curly doll hair in color desired
- ❑ Silver tinsel stem
- ❑ 8 (8mm) faceted acrylic stars in various colors
- ❑ 1½-inch (3.8cm) brass S hook
- ❑ 3 cups aquarium gravel
- ❑ Hot-glue gun

Stitching Step by Step

1 Following graphs (pages 10 and 11) throughout instructions, cut angel front, back, arms, wings front and back, book covers and book pages from plastic canvas. Back pieces for angel and wings will remain unstitched.

2 Stitch and assemble base pieces with soft navy, following General Instructions.

3 Stitch and Overcast arms. Stitch remaining pieces following graphs, working uncoded background on face with light peach Continental Stitches.

4 When background stitching is completed, work burgundy Backstitches for mouth and black floss Backstitches and Straight Stitches for eyelashes.

5 Whipstitch angel front and back together. Whipstitch wings front and back together.

6 Whipstitch wrong sides of book covers together along one 7-hole edge; Overcast remaining edges.

7 Whipstitch right sides of book pages together along one 6-hole edge; Overcast remaining edges.

Assembly

1 Use photo as a guide throughout assembly. Glue curly doll hair to angel as desired.

2 Glue wings to back of angel. Glue acrylic stars to robe where indicated on graph.

3 Glue elbow edges of arms to angel where indicated with brackets.

4 With wrong sides facing, center book pages over book cover; glue together. Fold book slightly in center, then glue cover to back side of hands, gluing bottom corners to angel.

5 Twist one end of silver tinsel stem into a halo with a stem, making halo about 1½ inches (3.8cm) in diameter. Trim stem to approximately 4½ inches (11.4cm). Glue stem to center back of wings.

6 Center and glue angel between front and back bases, making sure bottom edges are even.

7 Insert S hook in front center hole of base front top.

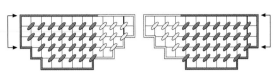

Arms
11 holes x 5 holes each
Cut 1 set

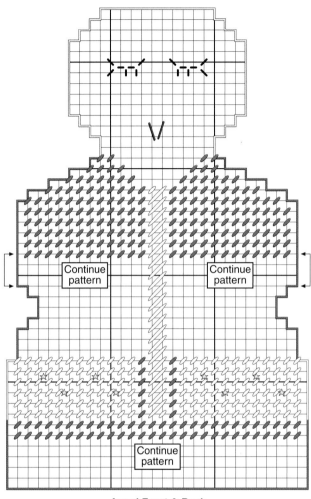

Angel Front & Back
29 holes x 45 holes
Cut 2
Stitch front only

Book Cover
6 holes x 7 holes
Cut 2

Book Page
5 holes x 6 holes
Cut 2

COLOR KEY	
Yards	**Medium Weight Yarn**
4 (3.7m)	☐ Light peach #257
11 (10.1m)	☐ White #311
3 (2.8m)	▨ Light gray #341
2 (1.9m)	■ Burgundy #376
42 (38.4m)	■ Soft navy #387
	Uncoded background on face is light peach #257 Continental Stitches
	✎ Burgundy #376 Backstitch
	6-Strand Embroidery Floss
1 (1m)	✎ Black Backstitch and Straight Stitch
	☆ Attach acrylic star

Color numbers given are for Red Heart Classic Art. E267 and Super Saver Art. E300 medium weight yarn.

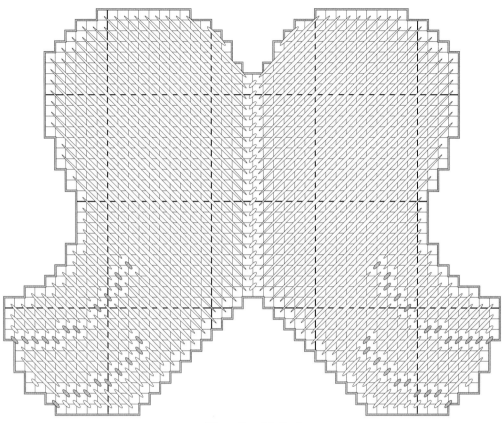

Wings Front & Back
48 holes x 38 holes
Cut 2
Stitch front only

Bear

Size: 5¾ inches W x 7½ inches H x 3⅞ inches D
(14.6cm x 19cm x 9.8cm)
Skill Level: Intermediate

Materials

❑ 2 sheets 7-count plastic canvas
❑ Red Heart Super Saver Art. E300 medium weight yarn as listed in color key
❑ Red Heart Classic Art. E267 medium weight yarn as listed in color key
❑ #16 tapestry needle
❑ Hand-sewing needle
❑ Black sewing thread
❑ ⁷⁄₁₆-inch (1.1cm) round black button
❑ ⅝-inch (1.6cm) dark red heart button
❑ 2 (7mm) round black cabochons
❑ 1½-inch (3.8cm) brass S hook
❑ 3 cups aquarium gravel
❑ Hot-glue gun

Stitching Step by Step

1 Following graphs. throughout instructions, cut bear front, back, arms, scarf tail and gift box from plastic canvas Bear back will remain unstitched.

2 Stitch and assemble base pieces with mid brown, following General Instructions.

3 Stitch bear front, working uncoded areas with mid brown Continental Stitches. Stitch and Overcast remaining pieces.

4 When background stitching is completed, work black Backstitches for mouth.

5 Use hand-sewing needle and black sewing thread to attach black button to head for nose where indicated on graph.

6 Using burgundy yarn, attach heart button to hat as in photo.

7 Whipstitch bear front and back together.

Assembly

1 Use photo as a guide throughout assembly. Glue cabochons to head for eyes where indicated on graph.

2 Center and glue bear between front and back bases, making sure bottom edges are even.

3 Tie a short length of white yarn in a bow and glue to gift box where indicated on graph, trimming tails as desired.

4 Center and glue gift box to bear. Glue arms in place. Glue scarf tail in place.

5 Insert S hook in front center hole of base front top.

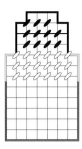

Arm
7 holes x 12 holes
Cut 2

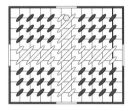

Gift Box
11 holes x 9 holes
Cut 1

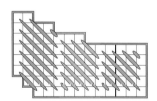

Scarf Tail
13 holes x 8 holes
Cut 1

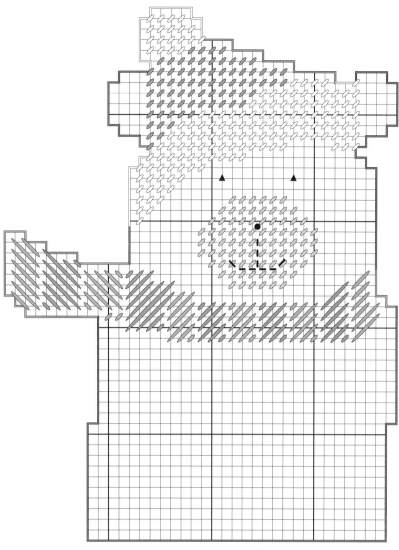

Bear Front & Back
38 holes x 50 holes
Cut 2
Stitch front only

COLOR KEY

Yards	Medium Weight Yarn
5 (4.6m)	☐ White #311
1 (1m)	■ Black #312
2 (1.9m)	☐ Warm brown #336
4 (3.7m)	☐ Paddy green #368
2 (1.9m)	☐ Burgundy #376
3 (2.8m)	☐ Skipper blue #848
40 (36.6m)	Uncoded areas are mid brown #339 Continental Stitches
╱	Mid brown #339 Overcast and Whipstitch
╱	Black #312 Backstitch
○	Attach white #311 bow
●	Attach black button
▲	Attach black cabochon

Color numbers given are for Red Heart Super Saver Art. E300 and Classic Art. E267 medium weight yarn.

Gingerbread Man

Size: 6⅞ inches W x 7½ inches H x 3⅞ inches D
(17.5cm x 19cm x 9.8cm)
Skill Level: Intermediate

Materials

- ❑ 2 sheets 7-count plastic canvas
- ❑ Red Heart Super Saver Art. E300 medium weight yarn as listed in color key
- ❑ Red Heart Classic Art. E267 medium weight yarn as listed in color key
- ❑ #16 tapestry needle
- ❑ 2 (⅝-inch/1.6cm) dark green heart buttons
- ❑ 2 (⅝-inch/1.6cm) dark red heart buttons
- ❑ 14 inches (35.6cm) ½-inch/0.5cm-wide white rickrack
- ❑ 2 (7mm) round black cabochons
- ❑ 1½-inch (3.8cm) brass S hook
- ❑ 3 cups aquarium gravel
- ❑ Hot-glue gun

Stitching Step by Step

1 Following graphs throughout instructions, cut gingerbread man front, back, hand and candy cane front and back from plastic canvas. Gingerbread man back and candy cane back will remain unstitched.

2 Stitch and assemble base pieces with warm brown, following General Instructions.

3 Stitch gingerbread man front and candy cane front, working uncoded areas with warm brown Continental Stitches. Stitch and Overcast hand.

4 When background stitching is completed, work burgundy Backstitches for mouth.

5 Using matching yarn, sew heart buttons to front between vest pieces where indicated on graph.

6 Whipstitch gingerbread man front and back together. Whipstitch candy cane front and back together.

Assembly

1 Use photo as a guide throughout assembly. Glue cabochons to head for eyes where indicated on graph.

2 Glue remaining dark green heart button to right side of hat.

3 Center and glue gingerbread man between front and back bases, making sure bottom edges are even.

4 Cut rickrack in two 4-inch (10.2cm) lengths and one 6-inch (15.2cm) length. Wrap and glue short lengths around hands. Wrap and glue longer length around front of gingerbread man just above front base, trimming ends as needed.

5 Glue candy cane in place; glue hand over candy cane at bottom of arm.

6 Insert S hook in front center hole of base front top.

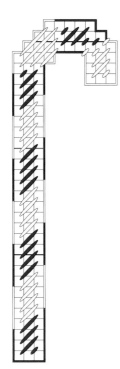

Candy Cane Front & Back
10 holes x 32 holes
Cut 2
Stitch front only

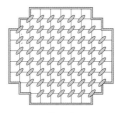

Hand
10 holes x 9 holes
Cut 1

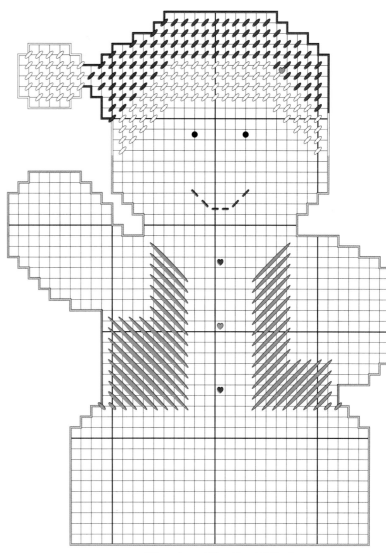

Gingerbread Man Front & Back
37 holes x 50 holes
Cut 2
Stitch front only

COLOR KEY

Yards	Medium Weight Yarn
5 (4.6m)	☐ White #311
46 (42.1m)	☐ Warm brown #336
5 (4.6m)	■ Burgundy #376
5 (4.6m)	■ Hunter green #389
	Uncoded areas are warm brown #336 Continental Stitches
╱	Burgundy #376 Backstitch
♥	Attach dark red heart button
♥	Attach dark green heart button
●	Attach black cabochon

Color numbers given are for Red Heart Super Saver Art. E300 and Classic Art. E267 medium weight yarn.

The full line of The Needlecraft Shop
products is carried by Annie's Attic catalog.
TOLL-FREE ORDER LINE
or to request a free catalog
(800) 582-6643
Customer Service
(800) 449-0440
Visit AnniesAttic.com

We have made every effort to ensure the accuracy
and completeness of these instructions. We cannot,
however, be responsible for human error, typographical
mistakes or variations in individual work.

ISBN: 978-1-57367-321-1

Printed in USA

1 2 3 4 5 6 7 8 9

Shopping for Supplies

For supplies, first shop your local craft
and needlework stores. Some supplies
may be found in fabric, hardware and
discount stores. If you are unable to find
the supplies you need, please call Annie's
Attic at (800) 582-6643 to request a free
catalog that sells plastic canvas supplies.

Before You Cut

Buy one brand of canvas for each entire project as brands can differ slightly in the distance between bars. Count holes carefully from the graph before you cut, using the bolder lines that show each 10 holes. These 10-count lines begin in the lower left corner of each graph to make counting easier. Mark canvas before cutting; then remove all marks completely before stitching. If the piece is cut in a rectangular or square shape and is either not worked, or worked with only one color and one type of stitch, the graph is not included in the pattern. Instead, the cutting and stitching instructions are given in the general instructions or with the individual project instructions.

Covering the Canvas

Bring needle up from back of work, leaving a short length of yarn on back of canvas; work over short length to secure. To end a thread, weave needle and thread through the wrong side of your last few stitches; clip. Follow the numbers on the small graphs beside each stitch illustration; bring your needle up from the back of the work on odd numbers and down through the front of the work on even numbers. Work embroidery stitches last, after the canvas has been completely covered by the needlepoint stitches.

Basic Stitches

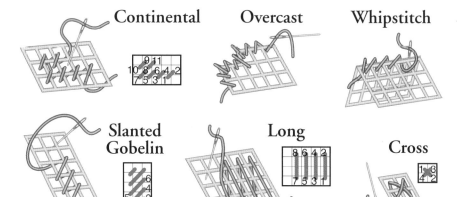

Embroidery Stitches

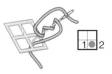

METRIC KEY:
millimeters = (mm)
centimeters = (cm)
meters = (m)
grams = (g)